About the authors

Vasilis Tsafas
Birth date: 7 August 1976
Place of birth: Axioupoli – Kilkis, Northern Greece
Occupation: In-service Officer (Civil Engineer) – Greek Air Force
Education: Hellenic Air Force Academy (BSc), City University London (MSc), Athens University of Economics and Business (MBA)

Dimitris Tsafas
Birth date: 7 December 1974
Place of birth: Axioupoli – Kilkis, Northern Greece
Occupation: Retired Officer (Captain) – Hellenic Navy Force

Education: Hellenic Navy Force Academy (BSc), Athens University of Economics and Business (MSc)

For us (Tsafas brothers), verse poetry (both in Greek and English) is not just a hobby. It's a passion that operates like psychotherapy, giving us the opportunity to express our souls out.

WOMAN: FRAGILE UNTIL SHE BREAKS...

Vasilis and Dimitris Tsafas

WOMAN: FRAGILE UNTIL SHE BREAKS...

Vanguard Press

VANGUARD PAPERBACK

© Copyright 2024 **Vasilis and Dimitris Tsafas**

The right of the **Vasilis and Dimitris Tsafas**
to be identified as authors of
this work has been asserted by them in accordance with the
Copyright, Designs and Patents Act 1988.

All Rights Reserved

No reproduction, copy or transmission of this publication
may be made without written permission.
No paragraph of this publication may be reproduced,
copied or transmitted save with the written permission of the
publisher, or in accordance with the provisions
of the Copyright Act 1956 (as amended).

Any person who commits any unauthorised act in relation to this
publication may be liable to criminal prosecution and civil claims for
damages.

A CIP catalogue record for this title is available from the British
Library.

ISBN 978-1-80016-984-5

This is a work of fiction. Names, characters, businesses, places, events and
incidents are either the products of the author's imagination or used in a
fictitious manner. Any resemblance to actual persons, living or dead, or actual
events is purely coincidental.

Vanguard Press is an imprint of
Pegasus Elliot Mackenzie Publishers Ltd.
www.pegasuspublishers.com

First Published in 2024

Vanguard Press
Sheraton House Castle Park
Cambridge England

Printed & Bound in Great Britain

Dedication

Dedicated to my wife, Elena V.T.
Dedicated to my niece, Evangelia D.T.

Acknowledgements

We would like to acknowledge and give our warmest thanks to the English teacher, Nadia Kehagia, whose support made this work possible. Her guidance and advice carried us through all the poems of this book.

Contents

MAN TO GOD	15
WOMAN (FRAGILE UNTIL SHE BREAKS)	17
I'M NOT A GREAT LOVER	19
HOLD ME TRASHED	20
DANCE ME ON AIRY STEPS	21
IT IS DOUBLE PLEASURE	23
MY E (MY EVANGELIA)	25
SHADOW IS THE PROOF	26
A SAINT HIDES THE PAST	27
PREY OR HUNTER	28
JUST A MOMENT IN A LIFETIME	30
GO IN SEARCH OF LIFE	31
UNFAIR DEBT	33
YOU HAVE TO DIE FIRST	34
HOLLY GAP	35
MY MAKER	36
ACCORDING TO	37
THAT WILL DO THE JOB	38
GO OFF ON ME	40

IT IS GOOD TO EXIST	42
YOU PLAY ME LIKE A VIDEO GAME	43
FEAR AND COURAGE	44
SET YOUR JOURNEY BY THE STARS	46
THE SMILE OF AN ANGEL	47
IN THE RIGHT HANDS (ELENA)	49
BETTER DAYS ARE ON THE WAY	51
FAR AWAY FROM TODAY	52
STOP LICKING YOUR WOUND	54
SOME DISTANCE FROM YOUR GRACE	56
MY MADNESS	57
TIME INDEPENDENT BEAUTY	58
REPEATED LIES	59
LET ME BE AN EYEWITNESS	60
PASSIVE DAYS	61
SLAVER OF YOUR FREEDOM	62
MY ENEMY IS MY MEMORY	63
THE SLIP	64
THE GREATEST THINGS	65
NEED TO PRY MY CAGE	66
EVERY NIGHT OF YOUR LIFE	68
THE STRONGEST TASTE	69

NO RESPONSE	71
O TEMPORA, O MORES	72
DAUGHTER OF THE MERCIFUL GOD	74
WITHOUT ME THERE IS NO I	76
A BEAUTY NEVER RIDES ITS BEAUTY	77
OH MOTHER (VAGELITSA)	79
SALVATION	81
I WANNA MAKE A CONFESSION	83
I'D RATHER BE SOMEONE ELSE	85
CITY STRAY HUMAN	87
BRAVER THAT DAY	88
DON'T ASK ME	90
ALL THE FIRST TIMES END	92
IN THE NIGHTS YOU ARE MINE	94
FLASHBACKS ECLIPSE THE MOON	96

MAN TO GOD

- Oh Lord, how can I experience paradise on Earth?
It seems to me so hard!

- My son, why are you confused?
I gave you paradise almost from the very first
   moment of your creation.
It's a part of you!

- Do You mean Woman?

- Exactly, the most beautiful creature I ever made!
She has the purest heart and the most creative mind.
The road to paradise goes through her.

- But our relationship is so complex.
Sometimes, I feel that Woman is the reason for my
   misery.

- The only reason for your misery is you, because
   you've forgotten your mission - to serve and treat
   her with love and respect.

- And what am I going to gain if I do so?

- Blissfulness!
You'll be rewarded with her graces, a true taste of heaven in this life.
But remember, she is fragile until she breaks, then cuts like a blade!

WOMAN (FRAGILE UNTIL SHE BREAKS)

After perfection, it is the end
Only imperfections keep us alive
Stop asking her to be something else
You're gonna taste the worst surprise

Her perfect version leads to an end
Do you understand?
Your end!

Fragile until she breaks
And then cuts like a blade
Ignoring your true feelings
She'll cut you in thousand pieces

Fragile until she breaks
And then cuts like a blade
No matter if looks churchy
She'll hurt you with no mercy

Difficult days could be a gift
Make a person better in minutes

Don't make her rise from her seat
If you don't wanna test her limits

A desperate day because of you
Will change her view
Of you!

I'M NOT A GREAT LOVER

Quiet hearts
Feed the loudest souls
In this silence
I am making songs
No matter what
They are entirely yours
You are the spring
Of all my thoughts

I'm not a great lover
But a man of great loves
It feels like a fight
Against our time
And against all odds

Deeper roots
Give the sweetest fruits
Although young
I prefer old suits
Retro shoes
I don't wear boots
Follow me
In the rhythm of blues

HOLD ME TRASHED

My love for you is still unexpressed
And this is why never dies
I have to deal with side effects
My comfort zone tells me lies

But I can feel it in my heart
A grey cloud is rising up
Over my soul during the nights
Blocking away the stellar lights

All my fears spring from the future
But my wounds are from the past
Need your hands to make me a suture
And your arms to hold me trashed

Translate my behavior
To alter my world
That's like standing water
Because I cannot

DANCE ME ON AIRY STEPS

This face is a gift from an ancient goddess
This body is a temple of mystic beliefs
A black-haired aura releases desires
Buried in thoughts of secret sweet sins

Only this beauty is driving me crazy
Only this motion is making me feel drugged
You've got such an impact on people's bright side
Your image could be a whole nation's flag

Jump in the air
Declare your freedom
Kick on the ground
Disdain the death
Bones and flesh
Of fathers' wisdom
Dance me, now,
On airy steps

This soul is a birth in ecstasy moments
This mind is a source of fantasy trips
An almond blue sight travels around
Spreading sensations of dangerous seas

Only this spirit is driving me crazy
Only this voice is making me feel drugged
You've got such an impact on people's bright side
Your image could be a whole nation's flag

IT IS DOUBLE PLEASURE

I have to say a lot
But I choose to stay quiet
No pauses or a dot
When you've cheated but deny it

I have to say a lot
But don't wanna interrupt you
Decisions and much more
Have been made but without you

It is double pleasure
That has no measure
To receive your lies
With a fake surprise

It is double pleasure
I feel no pressure
To observe your brow
While you make a vow

Enjoy your last speech
You can't repair the breach
I've gone off you, at last
The die has been cast

MY E (MY EVANGELIA)

Many years have passed
She was soft in my hands
Her small body, God's canvas
And for me, holly atlas

I was fully in a trance
Our moments went fast
How to sate my wishes
Couldn't ease my feelings

It seems like only yesterday
I think of my E every day
Condemned to this position
A never-ending mission

Smile my angel, smile
Your life is fragile
Cry your tears out
Your spirit wants to shout

SHADOW IS THE PROOF

How to win in love
When you lose in life
Trapped into a strife
With your own self

How to win in life
When you lose in love
Hiding in a hole
Like a strange elf

Your shadow is the proof
You're walking through the light
Don't waste precious time
Deforming who you are

Your shadow is the proof
You're human with emotions
With higher devotions
That shape what you are

How to win in love and life
With nobody by your side
Cause you think you couldn't have it
Most of all you don't deserve it

A SAINT HIDES THE PAST

You have to come to a decision
I don't deserve this competition
You better put this time an end
To my love or lovely friend

She doesn't want to see you happy
Investigating my sins
She tries to set your spirit crappy
Manipulating your wings

But I've been granted the concession
To make, at least, a true confession

A saint hides the past
While sinners call the future
The motive of my accuser
Revealed to you at last

The best suggestion can be heard
Is the advice of your heart
The vital drum's the only proof
Cause plays the rhythm of the truth

PREY OR HUNTER

I need to feel the love
The love of someone special
Who fits me like a glove
Releasing my potential

The money can't afford
The value of true feelings
Of course, I am sick of
Pretending fake healings

Boys are hunting
Girls are fishing
Prey or hunter
Both I'm wishing

I need to give my love
My love to someone beautiful
With beauty in the soul
I promise to be dutiful

Success is not enough
For happiness inside
Of course, I treat me rough
To appear satisfied

JUST A MOMENT IN A LIFETIME

Just a moment in a lifetime
Is enough to change the world
Your bright eyes were my lifeline
From the path you found me hurled

From the path you found me hurled
By the oaths, I kept alone
Mind trapped with broken wings
To cry out for a home

Just a moment in a lifetime
Is enough to fix the heart

Just a moment in a lifetime
Is enough to erase the cost
Your bright eyes were my lifeline
In the darkness, I was lost

In the darkness, I was lost
Cause of things proved to be fake
Giving up all of my dreams
Every step was a mistake

Just a moment in a lifetime
Is enough to fix the heart

GO IN SEARCH OF LIFE

It's a world given in pleasure
Mindsets of no measure
Narrow views keep us asleep
With illusions so deep

But you have the skills are needed
I can see you are completed
To escape from the fold
To create, from carbon, gold

Go in search of life
And you'll find the love you seek
Taste the sharpest knife
Better wounded than a meek

Go in search of life
To get what you're looking for
It's a time of strife
Answers bloom beyond your shore

It's not gonna be so easy
On the contrary, will be
Like a road that makes you wheezy

Like a desert with no tree

It's not gonna be so easy
But it's gonna set you free

UNFAIR DEBT

I paid a debt I didn't owe
Your glorious past I couldn't know
It's overwhelmed with psychic scars
That proved to be my erotic gaps

I took the rap of others' sins
You swore to love me by all means
I put my trust in the attraction
To your deceitful satisfaction

I paid a debt I didn't owe
I took the rap of others' sins
Cause all that every pain needs
Is just a victim for the show

It's my turn for passive action
Like a ring in a chain reaction
But I won't take your position
I'm gonna stray from this mission

YOU HAVE TO DIE FIRST

Don't hesitate to try
To spread your wings and fly
This world became major
By people with your nature

Don't be afraid to fail
Believing in a tale
This knowledge of the failures
Springs brilliant behaviors

If you wanna live
You have to die first
It's all about a trick
By life has been set

I was afraid to fight for my dreams
There was no chance to find my skills
But now things have changed and some more
Don't make the same mistakes, risk it all

HOLLY GAP

The weird time of breaking up
When space was empty
Your clout had left me
Some seconds proved my holly cap

It felt like I was an immortal
Yes, felt like nothing was important
Not even you, an inverse treason
A sudden sense with no reason

I tried to explain these flying birds
Impossible to find the words
Unleashed my body and my soul
I'm gonna let the life roll

So, don't be sorry
Don't
You have to worry
Not
Our breaking up
Has woken up
Perspectives for new glory

MY MAKER

You are the maker of my mistakes
I'll pay the cost whatever it takes
You're also right, the blame is mine
I never traced a full red line

You are the maker of my new life
I've learned from you how to survive
Under unfair circumstances
How to find second chances

From your errors, I corrected my own
I'm not wise but a victim who has flown
Flesh and bones that have grown

My love is more important than your words
They have taught me how to spend it for a cause
Every cloud is a block before the sun
Sunny days, now I know, are yet to come

ACCORDING TO

You have an image to maintain
There is no time to proclaim
Such silly things as the affairs
Among your race, nobody cares

I have my self-worth to develop
It doesn't matter if I had hoped
You might be my alter ego
That hope was only a placebo

My feelings for you
Are according to yours
Some kind of win
Or a kind of loss

What made you think we are the same
My beating heart defines my name
In contradiction to your life
That's pushed around as though is blind

THAT WILL DO THE JOB

I didn't climb your stairs
Because I was helpless
But honestly, I'm just wondering
If you could be more selfless

I need you in my life
I smile when you smile
We're candid with each other, so
I'm asking cause I have to know
"Can you be really mine?"

I didn't ask for water
Because I was thirsty
But honestly, I'm just wondering
If you could act with mercy

I need to say these words
I see two different worlds
We're candid with each other, so
I'm asking cause I have to know
"Can I be really yours?"

Show me that you want me
Let me touch your body
That will do the job until
You tell me that you love me

GO OFF ON ME

Relentless anger grows in your chest
A big confusion takes on your mind
Cause every first time seems to be the best
But in the end, it only sets you blind

A thousand thoughts decay in your head
Your smiling face is gonna be postponed
The only thing you dream of is a land
Where no flower ever stood alone

Love is the treatment
Makes you fly higher
Impart your secret
Claim your desire

Go off on me

You feel it's difficult to change inside
But I'm here for you
I'll be here for you

You think it's easier to run and hide
But I'm here for you

IT IS GOOD TO EXIST

I was wrong and you were right
Always right, always strong
My mistakes made me grow
For the one that I love

I was small before your feelings
Didn't know what I want
The fallout made me grow
For the one that I love

And the one that I love
It is you, my perfect lover
Please forgive me if nothing's over

It is good to exist
But to live is much better
So, I wrote this letter
To your heart, I've missed

It is good to exist
But to live is much better
And I thought doesn't matter
If you insist to resist

YOU PLAY ME LIKE A VIDEO GAME

You play me like a video game
You treat me with a lazy wrist
My keys are marked with your byname
My easy days don't exist

Push the button, put an end
Put an end to my weakness
Push the one is colored red
And I'll give you my forgiveness

I feel I am a loaded trigger
I think I'm ready to explode
My life circled by your finger
Is trapped in anything you want

Pull the trigger, make me vent
Make me vent to find freedom
Pull it firmly, no regret
And will be an act of wisdom

FEAR AND COURAGE

Challenges
Of different realities
Savages
Surrendered to their fantasies
Honestly
There's nothing to explain
Hopefully
Your dreams are not in vain

Totally
Afraid to speak openly
Probably
Because of your probity
Loneliness
Protects you from the phonies
More or less
You had to make this choice

Fear is a reaction
But courage is the action
Break these inner burning chains
To find your satisfaction

Fear is a reaction
But courage is the action
Let the risk run through your veins
And you will gain traction

SET YOUR JOURNEY BY THE STARS

The advice I could give you by heart
You may think is not a real piece of art
But, it's coming straight through from my mistakes
So, to you, I'm gonna give my better takes

The advice I could give you, my love
It's above our common future and beyond
Cause believe me if it's meant to be together
Should be ready for all kinds of odd weather

I don't wanna feign your master
I've just seen inside the monster

Set your journey by the stars
Not the lights of passing cars
Follow instincts made of soul
Not main streams under control

THE SMILE OF AN ANGEL

I need no tears to cry
No real wings to fly
A secret world inside me
Is spreading like a sea

I need no pain to pray
No power to play
A different zest inside me
Is blowing like a wind

The smile of an angel
On your devilish face
This beauty makes you a stranger
Who is taking your place

This smile of an angel
Just two dangerous lines
Your beauty makes me unable
To deny the signs

I keep my pace slow
My eyes always low
A selfish world inside you
Is out of my view

I keep myself away
From everything you say
A greedy zest inside you
Is hunting like a wolf

IN THE RIGHT HANDS (ELENA)

Raw material from the earth
Is the beauty of your face
That provokes divine mirth
So unknown to our race

Passing comets through the sky
Are the movements of your lips
For the men are going by
The whole world is in eclipse

In the right hands
You'll bloom like a flower
With a perfume power
That can drug the gods

Wish I were a blind beggar
At the door of your bodega
Drinking sips of Spanish wine
With no cost from your red vine

Wish I had the sharpest claws
In a city with no laws
To sweat blood for your attention
For your pricey affection

BETTER DAYS ARE ON THE WAY

Who was ever wise by chance?
Wisdom comes with failure as a reason
Fading scars of any circumstance
Tell the tale of every painful season

Who was ever happy on his own?
Happiness demands a real connection
In this crazy world, we're not alone
Everybody is starving for affection

Better days are on the way
Dreaming makes the soul rotate
From my darkness to your light
Only you are on my mind

Even the echo of your voice is enough
To make me smile while things are getting rough
Even the shadow of your body is too strong
To make me feel like I'm protected from a storm

FAR AWAY FROM TODAY

I'm sitting on my knees
What kind of view is this?
You're closing the door
You leave me all alone

You leave me high and dry
I have no tears to cry
No time for begging words
This moment is for thoughts

I'm thinking of myself
It's hard to understand
The emptiness I live
Convicting me of guilt

You leave me high and dry
I have no strengths to try
The promised fit of anger
Although I feel the hunger

But I know one day
In a silly prose
You will write you chose
The most senseless way

And I know that day
Should be far away
From today

STOP LICKING YOUR WOUND

I see in my dreams
An angel with broken wings
It sings to me a song
About a never lasting love

The voice is so deep
That seems to be a fey weep
The feeling is so strong
That makes me think all day long

If you wanna be cured
Stop licking your wound
If you wanna live fast
Stop touching your scars
Only time belongs to us

We've got the strength to go too far
A wish is just a falling star
The perfect life doesn't worth
The secret is to move it forth

If you wanna be cured
Stop licking your wound
If you wanna be loved
Start opening more
Only time can close the door

SOME DISTANCE FROM YOUR GRACE

I don't know who I am
I've lost my faith in me
A pawn in your game
I used to be the king

I don't know what I want
I'm totally confused
My thoughts have been blocked
My feelings are abused

Give me time, only time
I am trying to survive
Give me space, my space
I need distance from your grace

Some distance from your grace
To clean my painted face

MY MADNESS

My madness, yes this madness
Discovered her sobriety
That lights up the darkness
Forgiving all my vanity

There is no ounce of regret
No second thoughts to forget
I'm not the same anymore
She made me change to the core

There is no chance of retreat
The fight scars are so sweet
I wanna come to an end
Either alive or dead

There is no ounce of regret
Or any chance of retreat
I'm living things didn't get
To catch the springs used to jilt

TIME INDEPENDENT BEAUTY

Time independent beauty
I can see it in your eyes
Something weird travels through me
Reaching up to cloudy skies

I don't mean your perfect face
Neither talk about your body
You belong to an alien race
That is touching down upon me

I just mean your chainless spirit
Has been spread with gently gestures
There's no hitch or any limit
That could subdue your expressions

Unseen characteristics
Perceivable by instincts
I hope you understand me
I'm lost in my feelings

REPEATED LIES

Repeated lies became the truth
The substitute for any proof
The sun is rising from the west
I'm all alone in this mess

My heartbeat's gonna be replaced
By city sounds in a race
My soul, betrayed by yours
Is getting tough behind the doors

It fails, falls and breaks
But then it heals and overcomes
No matter what it takes
I'll fix once more my gammy thumbs
To hit again my dusty drums

Repeated lies became the truth
I wanna jump down from the roof
To set me free among the winds
To feel my soul spreading its wings

LET ME BE AN EYEWITNESS

Only pain can break the weakness
Only pain can make you strong
Let me be an eyewitness
When the moment comes along

This is how my love looks like
This is how I'll stand by you
Come with me and join my ride
For a different point of view

Don't forget to pack your stories
Don't forget to bring your past
The adventure eases worries
As the day passes fast

Gloomy daughter
Take my offer
Trust my intentions
No conventions

PASSIVE DAYS

I've never missed the mornings
That I used to wake up
With a smile on the heart

I've never missed the warnings
That I used to overlook
Cause I'd lost my mind on you

Now I'm running passive days
Orphan days of your blaze
But at least my soul is peaceful
Loading up from scratch my pistol

It's so hard to say "I regret you"
I am trying to forget you
Wishing on a solid rung
While this life is still young

SLAVER OF YOUR FREEDOM

Fight for the life you want
In this world, you are alone
Light the fire you dreamed of
Everybody's on his own

Second thoughts, bare of vision
End up soon to a bad decision
Nothing else can make you wise
Only stories of surprise

On the other side of fear
There's the edge of a new kingdom
You just have to admit right here
You're the slaver of your freedom

Measured words
Stricken chords
Bullied mind
Turns aside
From the pride

MY ENEMY IS MY MEMORY

My enemy is my memory
Absorbs my whole energy
I'm patient in lethargy

My clinic is my residence
Because of my hesitance
To face all the evidence

But nothing is more absolute
That I was only a substitute
For your decay in solitude

The limits of my nature
Have been in days of danger
My image shows a stranger

Your impact I am buffering
White nights bring me suffering
Takes time this recovering

THE SLIP

I was such a fool
Thinking of love be only a tool
I was such a scum
Thinking of sins be drowned in rum
In this hunt for truth
Needed to waste the best of my youth
But if time is up
Show me a sign I have to give up

Just try to understand
The slip that brought me to your hands
Please, try to forgive
The slip that brought me to your feet

Already I've said enough
Already I see I'm back from the dark
But something's missing inside my chest
So nothing gives me rest

THE GREATEST THINGS

I feel it in my bones
I'm crashing all my fears
Between converting stones
A bubbling storm over the sea
Is revving up "my wants"

I feel it on my skin
I'm thinking of my future
In terms of fulfilled sins
The grey sky above the streets
Is revving up my needs

The greatest things
Always begin
From my broken heart
Which needs a hell
To suit me well
From the very start

Don't try to kiss me, I hate your lips
You waste your time, I know your tricks
I've been true darkness, not eclipse
Don't try to fix me, I can't be fixed

NEED TO PRY MY CAGE

All the shadows from the past
Have been gone
I have left them back

Every scar and every bruise
Are my muse
They have cut me loose

Now it's time for me to change
Need to pry my cage
Even though I have to strive
To check bones on the knife

I have worked on this a lot
At my spot
An erratic plot

Every beating of my heart
By far
Is a piece of art

I'm not trying to make it even
I have set myself forgiven
By me, my life is driven

EVERY NIGHT OF YOUR LIFE

Dressed up as a junkie
Acting like an angel
I can see you're hungry
For a brand new danger

Living in the illusion
Of the hero ranger
I can see your fusion
With a brand new stranger

Every night of your life
Is the story of a strife
Cut off dreams by a carving knife

But there is a weird feeling
All your scars with no deep healing
Seem to me so much appealing

To be honest with myself
Wish I were like you as well
Wish I'd met you years ago
Cause you make my spirit blow

THE STRONGEST TASTE

Give me your hand
Don't be afraid
I'm gonna show you how to survive

I'm just a friend
Open the gate
Your broken heart is still alive

Listen to me
I'll set you free
I've lived the storm, without being warned

If you go against yourself
Then you go against your fate
But our fate always wins
So we can't avoid the bait
Since being born, it is too late

Sometimes love goes to waste
It's the strongest taste
Show me your scars
Don't hesitate
I wanna tell you how to treat them

Under the stars
The mind state
Turns to a sea where all are forgiven

Listen to you
This beat is true
Inside your chest, without some rest

NO RESPONSE

I'm not pretending
No response can be a powerful one
A useless myriad of words
Before the beating of a heart

I have been lost in thoughts of grief
Of promises, I don't believe
The answers you are looking for
Volatilize me to the core

I loved you more than anything
With all of my trust
I gave you almost everything
That's why I'm getting crushed

I loved you more than anything
I gave you almost everything
And now I'm feeling bust

I'm not pretending "no response"
But silence comes to be the most
Expressive way to vent my screams
Left high and dry by your dreams

O TEMPORA, O MORES

The worst years were the best
Instead of high technology
A blooming psychology
Surrounded by friends

The worst years were the best
With no career pride
With you by my side
Free from social trends

O tempora, o mores
After all this progress
We failed to succeed
Given in to speed

O tempora, o mores
After all this progress
We failed to be loved
Used to be shoved

The best years are the worst
Addicted to materials
Consuming TV serials
The most of us are lost

The best years are the worst
Unable to care
Incapable to share
We ignore the line we crossed

DAUGHTER OF THE MERCIFUL GOD

One way ticket
Not by choice
You're not prepared
For the sky silver noise

After some days
The first full stop
A filthy camp
Away from the so much wanted hope

During the nights
Tragic men
Come to your shelter
Again and again and again

In almost nine months
You'll not be alone
Your body is changing
A new life is about to born

Don't be afraid
From now and on
You're not just a woman
But daughter of the merciful God

Freedom is close
A boat in the sea
The water is hungry
Its color, mysteriously deep

End of the journey
Wasn't so long
Rest in peace
Daughter of the merciful God

WITHOUT ME THERE IS NO I

Me and I
No matter how hard I try
It's always me who makes me cry
The blame is mine

Me and I
Nobody knows about this conflict
I'm all alone into an orbit
How to stop it?

Without me there is no I
I've got the strength to give the fight
Without me there is no I
I'm gonna bring me light

So easy for myself to judge me
No matter if I always hurt me
Supposed I'm getting a better person
I feel trapped in this situation
Have I learned my lesson?

A BEAUTY NEVER RIDES ITS BEAUTY

Socializing cultured savages
Spirits full of modern damages
Stilted faces in the streets
I'm a beast among the beasts

In this desperate situation
An unconscious transformation
I was hit by your forces
My life's blazing torches

Virtues mixed in nature's multi
Synthesized you to mute me
What a great sense of duty
You refuse to ride your beauty

Eye candy makes me hungry
How to control my body
I'm supposed to be dandy
So ashamed but still, randy

Socializing sly characters
All the kinds of prizefighters
Fodder pawns with no rules
Was a fool among the fools

From this vain situation
An unwelcome deformation
I got free by your eyes
My life's guide lights

OH MOTHER (VAGELITSA)

When a new life comes in the world
A woman also is reborn
Her life changes forever
But she's more beautiful than ever

In case of need
She's always there
It's like whispering a prayer
"Oh mother
Everything is going fast
Come and ease me with your touch
Missed you much

Oh mother
I'm afraid of this world
I can't fight them anymore
Make me strong

Oh mother
Only you can fix my stings
Only you piece by piece
Make them cease"

When a new life comes in the world
A woman also is reborn
Plenty of feelings in her chest
She never rests but feels so blessed

SALVATION

Love me only for my youth
Free your wishes

Bones and flesh that look so good
Feed your instincts

Love me now with an end
You're not an angel

I know commitments make you mad
Accept your nature

Salvation is out of the book
Take a short look
Salvation is standing on the edge
Be a savage

Love me only cause I'm young
I also want it

Long term love is not enough
Life taught me

No mistakes and no regrets
It's my protection

The mirror always reprimands
Our soul's reflection

I WANNA MAKE A CONFESSION

I wanna make a confession
Please, give me all of your attention

Loneliness's my strongest fear
I'm so happy that you're here
Seems to be the answer
To this cancer, my dear

I wanna make a confession
Please, give me all of your attention

Sharing is my biggest need
Life was lavish with my feed
Seems to be some testing
For this blessing, I received

I do anything for love
But, my love

If this feeling doesn't go both ways
If the need for giving doesn't run the gaze
Common future ends up in a total mess

Looks more like dealing than true healing
Deep inside our chest

I'D RATHER BE SOMEONE ELSE

Once in a while in my dreams
A visitor is coming
With no expression on his face
Is waiting for something

He is familiar to me
Same eyes same nose
With no need of any talk
We make the same thoughts

"I'd rather be someone else
Someone else who'd rather be me
If only I could love myself
More in a way that I deserve

I'd rather be someone else
Someone else who'd rather be me
If only I could see myself
Close but out of mind's shell"

Once in a while in my dreams
A guest takes position
He doesn't smile he doesn't speak
Is there for a reason

He is familiar to me
Same fears same worries
With no need of any talk
We make the same stories

CITY STRAY HUMAN

There's no home to get rest
No workplace to be stressed
Always free to live your life
No matter what is right

There's no need to be somebody
No dreams about money
Always happy with yourself
Born to be an urban elf

Labeled outcast by the system
Cause you're dancing off its rhythm

City stray human
You're the future we're afraid of
City stray human
But you're really what we pray for

City stray human
You are everything we wanna be
City stray human
Truth's upon you for the rest to see

BRAVER THAT DAY

Her name's unimportant
She is living with her dog
She likes spending money
On books and that is all

He feels like a nonentity
He's living all alone
Quite boring days
But life's going on

She pays the book in haste
She walks the street with grace
He bangs into her softly
She didn't back up off him

Goodbye in their eyes
Same thoughts in their mind

"Oh my angel, love should wait
Till I fall on you again
I'll be braver that day"

So hard to be expressed
What was reflected in their glance
There was only one chance

DON'T ASK ME

Don't ask me who I am
I've no idea
My whole past insists to have
The shape of my tear

Don't ask me what I am
You better never know
The hidden secrets in my soul
Are footprints on the snow

Don't ask me how I feel
I hate to explain
With actions in all sizes
I write my name

Don't ask me what I think
My thoughts an endless story
The mind's used to block the heart
With days of past glory

You say it's OK
To play with me this game
Get ready for the answer
You're gonna see a monster

ALL THE FIRST TIMES END

I could live with her forever
I was happier than ever
Our love was quite enough
But for her, conversely tough

And she felt the need for change
Wanted things out of my range
Soon this change knocked the door
And it dragged her by the soul

All the first times end
It's called fate, my friend
Every first time's short
Leaving thoughts of hurt

I could see this moment coming
My dreams were keeping humming
But I wanted to believe
There was no cause to grieve

And the dreams proved to be real
Nothing's ever ideal
That's my story more or less
And the reason for my mess

IN THE NIGHTS YOU ARE MINE

A day away is the moon
Its light gives me hope
A red inflated balloon
I'm hanging on its rope

Your love was never easy
Your kiss was always breezy
And memories are coming back
Like lucid dreams to please me

In the nights you are mine
Till the morning, on my mind
In my heart, I've set you free
From the things you're forced to be

A day away is the stars
Their light makes me smile
I feel no pain from my scars
My thoughts are reconciled

Your spirit was agile
Your happiness fragile
Because of this, my whole world
Is signed by your style

FLASHBACKS ECLIPSE THE MOON

The impact of your absence
I'm trying to calculate
In order to escape
From my cage of silence

In this quiet madness
The sins can't be forgiven
Behaviors are driven
By beliefs or violence

Perhaps it is too late
To set from scratch my fate
Perhaps it is too soon
Flashbacks eclipse the moon

The impact of your absence
In this quiet madness
Looks like a cage of silence
The air smells self-violence